IS-907 – ACTIVE SHOOTER: WHAT YOU CAN DO

This course has been developed by the National Protection and Programs Directorate/Office of Infrastructure Protection, U.S. Department of Homeland Security, and is being hosted by the Emergency Management Institute (EMI).

For more information or to address questions or comments about this course, please contact IP_Education@HQ.dhs.gov

COURSE INTRODUCTION

Visual 1

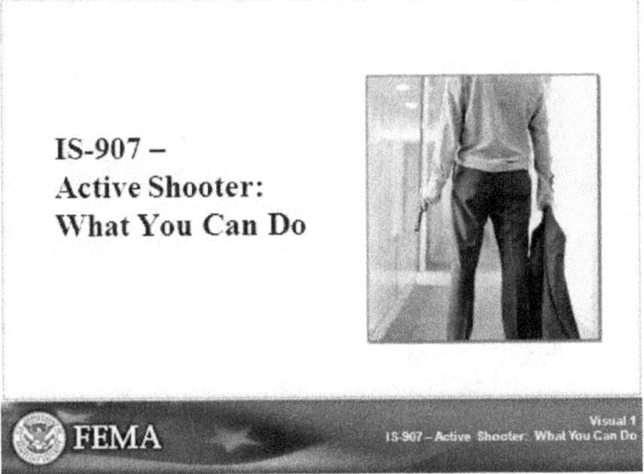

Key Points

Welcome to the Active Shooter course. This course provides guidance to help you prepare to respond to an active shooter situation.

COURSE INTRODUCTION

Visual 2

Key Points

COURSE INTRODUCTION

Visual 3

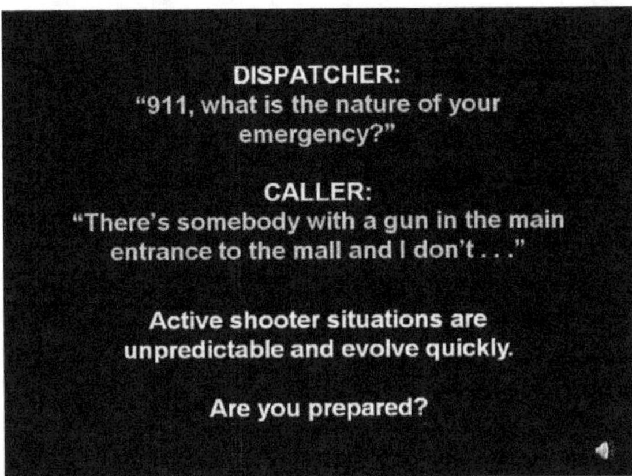

Key Points

Dispatcher: "911, what is the nature of your emergency?"

Caller: "There's somebody with a gun in the main entrance to the mall and I don't . . ."

Are you prepared?

COURSE INTRODUCTION

Visual 4

Key Points

By the end of this course, you will be able to:

- Describe actions to take when confronted with an active shooter and with law enforcement officials who are responding to the situation.
- Recognize potential workplace violence indicators.
- Describe actions to take to prevent and prepare for potential active shooter incidents.
- Describe how to manage the consequences of an active shooter incident.

Not all recommendations provided here will be applicable at every facility. This course is intended to provide guidance to enhance facility-specific plans and procedures.

COURSE INTRODUCTION

Visual 5

Key Points

During the past several years, there have been many active shooter incidents:

- **Where we shop.** In 2007 a gunman killed 5 and injured multiple others at a Utah mall.
- **Where we exercise our free speech.** In 2011 U.S. Representative Gabrielle (Gabby) Giffords was critically shot while meeting with constituents at a market, with 6 people killed and 3 others injured.
- **Where we learn.**
  - In 1999 at Columbine High School 12 students and 1 teacher were killed.
  - In 2007 at Virginia Tech 32 were killed and many others wounded.
  - In 2008 at Northern Illinois University 5 students were killed.
- **Where we work.** In 2010 a gunman opened fire at a beer distributor, killing 8 people.

Most active shooter situations are unpredictable and evolve quickly. Because most incidents are over within minutes, we must be prepared to deal with the situation until law enforcement personnel arrive.

Preparedness and awareness are the keys to helping protect our employees, our customers, and ourselves.

COURSE INTRODUCTION

Visual 6

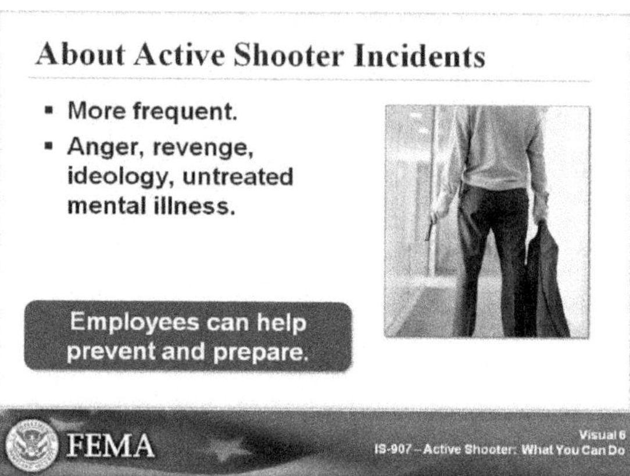

Key Points

Active shooter incidents are becoming more frequent.

Common motives include anger, revenge, ideology, and untreated mental illness.

All employees can help prevent and prepare for potential active shooter situations.

COURSE INTRODUCTION

Visual 7

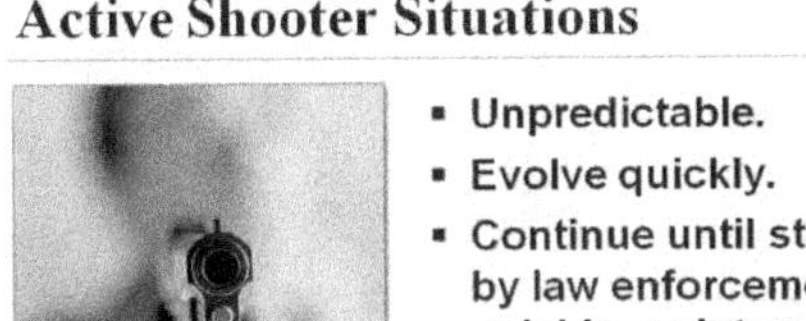

Key Points

An active shooter is an individual actively engaged in killing or attempting to kill people in a confined space or other populated area. In most cases, active shooters use firearms and there is no pattern or method to their selection of victims.

Active shooter situations are unpredictable and evolve quickly.

Active shooters usually will continue to move throughout a building or area until stopped by law enforcement, suicide, or other intervention. Typically, the deployment of law enforcement is required to stop the shooting and to prevent further harm to victims.

COURSE INTRODUCTION

Visual 8

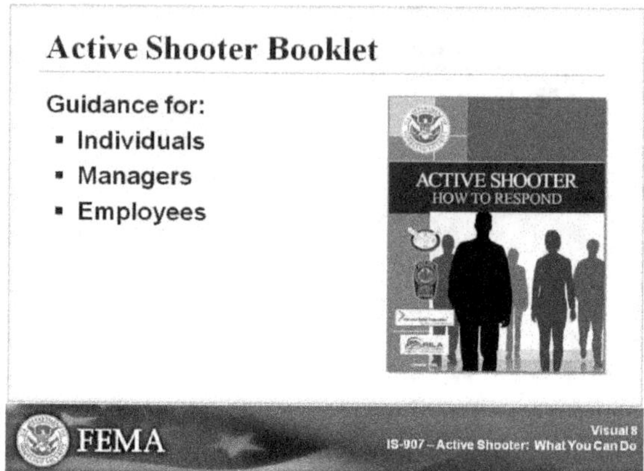

Key Points

The information presented in this course is summarized in the booklet titled **"Active Shooter: How To Respond"** (http://www.dhs.gov/xlibrary/assets/active_shooter_booklet.pdf), published by the U.S. Department of Homeland Security.

This booklet provides guidance to individuals, including managers and employees, who may become involved in an active shooter situation, and discusses how to react when law enforcement responds.

The booklet can also be downloaded from the **course Web site** (http://training.fema.gov/EMIWeb/IS/IS907.asp), which you will access to take the final exam.

RESPOND

Visual 9

Key Points

The remainder of this course is divided into the following sections:

- Respond
- Prepare
- Follow Up

This section of the course covers response actions, including how to respond when law enforcement arrives.

RESPOND

Visual 10

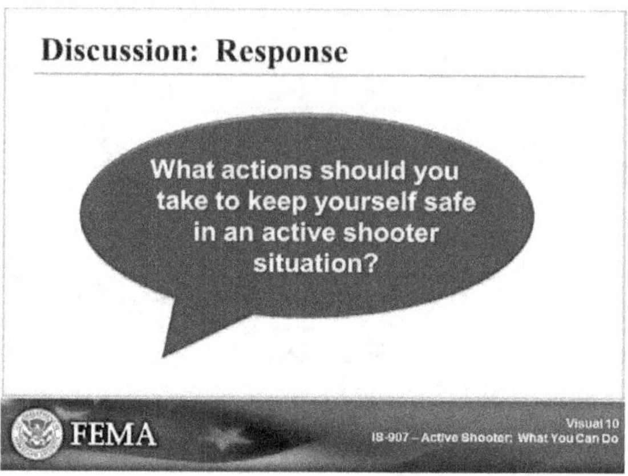

Key Points

What response actions should you take to keep yourself safe in an active shooter situation?

RESPOND

Visual 11

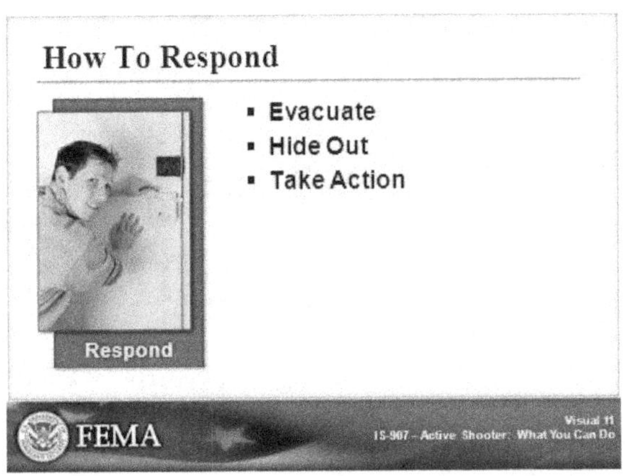

Key Points

In an active shooter situation, all involved persons should quickly determine the most reasonable way to protect their own lives.

Recommended actions, in order, are:

- **Evacuate:** If there is an accessible escape path, attempt to evacuate the premises.
- **Hide out:** If evacuation is not possible, find a place to hide where the active shooter is less likely to find you.
- **Take action:** As a last resort, and if your life is in imminent danger, attempt to disrupt and/or incapacitate the active shooter.

Training is important to enable you to react appropriately if confronted with an active shooter situation. As these situations evolve quickly, quick decisions could mean the difference between life and death. If you are in harm's way, you will need to decide rapidly what the safest course of action is based on the scenario that is unfolding.

RESPOND

Visual 12

Evacuate (1 of 2)

- Have an escape route and plan in mind.
- Leave your belongings behind.
- Help others escape, if possible.
- Evacuate regardless of others.
- Warn/prevent individuals from entering.

Key Points

The first recommended action is to evacuate. If there is an accessible escape path, attempt to evacuate the premises.

When evacuating:

- Have an escape route and plan in mind.
- Leave your belongings behind.
- Help others escape, if possible.
- Evacuate regardless of whether others agree to follow.
- Warn individuals not to enter an area where the active shooter may be.
- Prevent individuals from entering an area where the active shooter may be.

(Continued on the following page.)

RESPOND

Visual 13

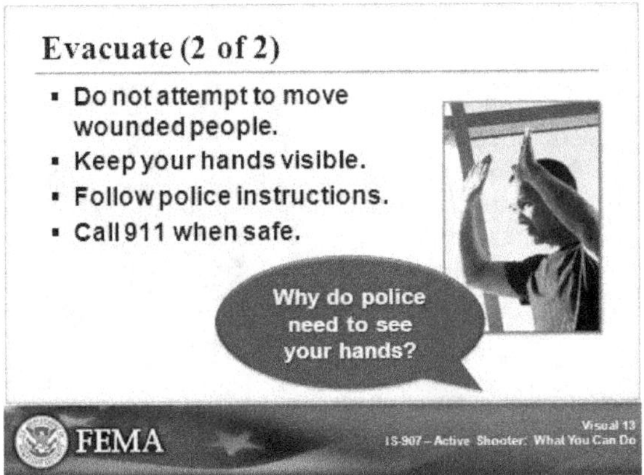

Key Points

When evacuating (continued):

- Do not attempt to move wounded people.
- Keep your hands visible.
- Follow the instructions of any police officers.
- Call 911 when it is safe to do so.

Why do police officers need to see your hands when you exit the premises in an active shooter situation?

RESPOND

Visual 14

Key Points

The next recommended action is to hide out. If safe evacuation is not possible, find a place to hide from the active shooter.

The hiding place should:

- Be out of the active shooter's view.
- Provide protection if shots are fired (for example, an office with a closed and locked door).
- Not restrict options for movement.

To prevent an active shooter from entering a hiding place:

- Lock the door.
- Blockade the door with heavy furniture. This also provides additional protection.
- Close, cover, and move away from any windows.

RESPOND

Visual 15

Key Points

If the active shooter is nearby, take the following actions:

- Lock the door.
- Hide behind a large item (for example, a cabinet or desk).
- Silence your cell phone and/or pager. (Even the vibrate setting can give away a hiding position.)
- Remain quiet.

Consider the difference between cover and concealment. Cover might protect a person from gunfire, while concealment will merely hide a person from the view of the shooter.

Persons in an active shooter situation should quickly choose the best space that is available. Finding cover is preferable, but if cover is not available you should find a position of concealment.

RESPOND

Visual 16

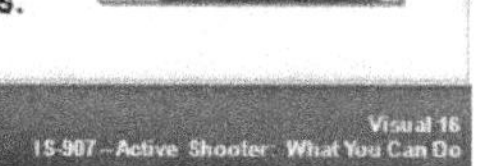

Key Points

When possible, provide the following information to law enforcement officers or 911 operators:

- Location of the active shooter.
- Number of shooters, if more than one.
- Physical description of the shooter(s).
- Number and type of weapons held by the shooter(s).
- Number of potential victims at the location.

RESPOND

Visual 17

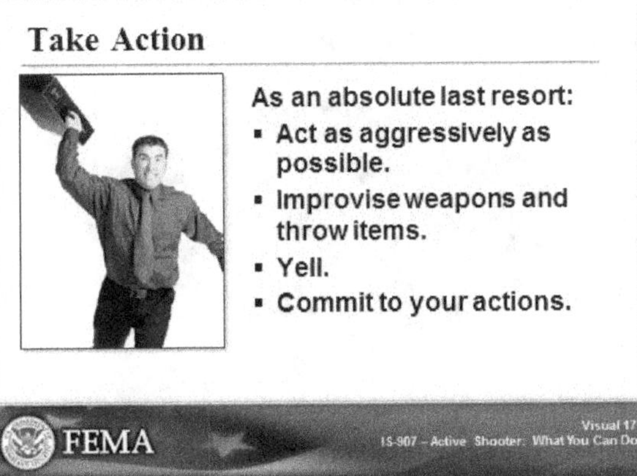

Key Points

Finally, as an absolute last resort, and only if in imminent danger, attempt to disrupt and/or incapacitate the active shooter.

- Act as aggressively as possible.
- Improvise weapons and throw items.
- Yell.
- Commit to your actions.

RESPOND

Visual 18

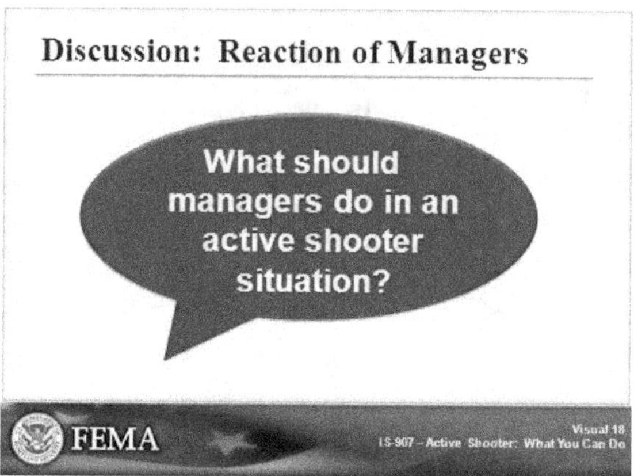

Key Points

What should managers do in an active shooter situation?

ACTIVITY: WHAT WOULD YOU DO?

Visual 19

Key Points

Activity Purpose: To reinforce your understanding of how best to prepare for and respond to an active shooter situation.

Instructions: Working as a team:

1. Look around the room you are in. Consider what you would do in an active shooter situation and whether it would be better to escape or hide.
2. Come up with a list of the actions you would take to protect yourself and those around you.
3. Record the list on chart paper.
4. Select a spokesperson and be prepared to present the list in 5 minutes.

RESPOND

Visual 20

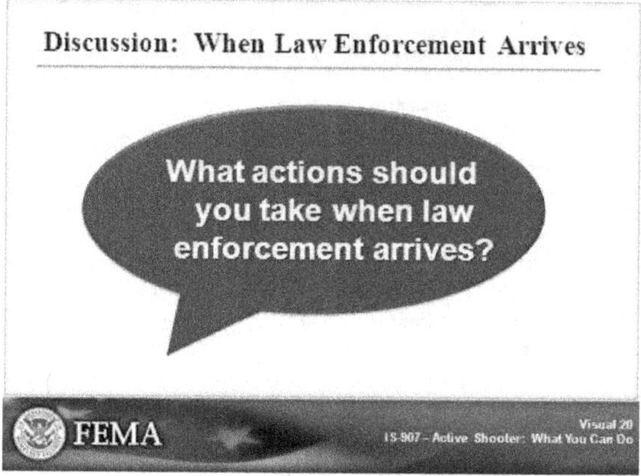

Key Points

What actions should you take when law enforcement arrives?

RESPOND

Visual 21

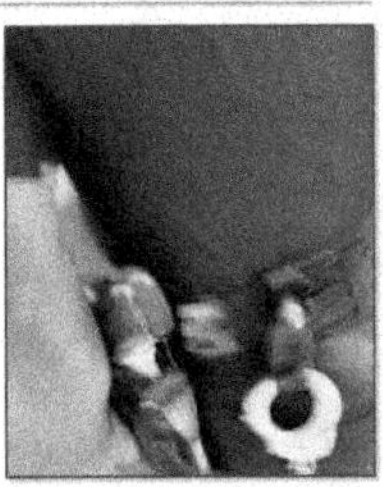

Key Points

When law enforcement officers arrive at an active shooter scene:

- Their immediate purpose is to stop the active shooter as soon as possible.
- Officers will proceed directly to the area in which the last shots were heard.
- The first officers to arrive at the scene will not stop to help injured persons because their first priority is to eliminate the threat. They will need to secure the scene first.

When there is an emergency such as an active shooter incident, it is important to remember that officers arriving on scene may be coming from many different duty assignments and will likely be in various types of uniforms and even in street clothes. Do not be surprised by the variations in appearance, as law enforcement personnel are trained to react quickly and work together.

RESPOND

Visual 22

Key Points

Additional officers may arrive in teams, such as a SWAT (special weapons and tactics) team.

These teams may:

- Wear regular patrol uniforms or external bulletproof vests, Kevlar helmets, and other tactical equipment. Some officers may be in plain clothes.
- Be armed with rifles, shotguns, or handguns.
- Use pepper spray or tear gas to control the situation.
- Shout commands, and push individuals to the ground for their safety.

Emergency medical personnel will also arrive at the scene. Rescue teams will treat and remove any injured persons. These teams may request able-bodied individuals to assist in removing the wounded from the premises.

RESPOND

Visual 23

Key Points

Recommended actions to take when law enforcement officers arrive are listed on the visual.

RESPOND

Visual 24

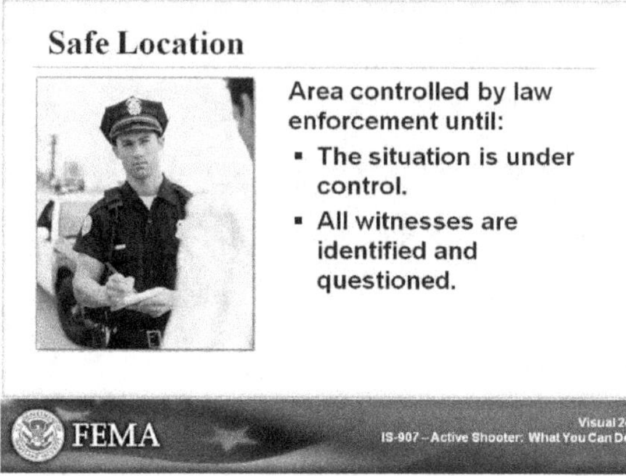

Key Points

After reaching a safe location or assembly point, all persons involved in the situation likely will be held in that area by law enforcement until the situation is under control, and all witnesses have been identified and questioned.

No one should leave the safe location or assembly point until law enforcement authorities indicate it is safe and their questioning has been completed.

PREPARE

Visual 25

Key Points

This section of the course covers actions to take to prepare for and prevent potential active shooter incidents.

PREPARE

Visual 26

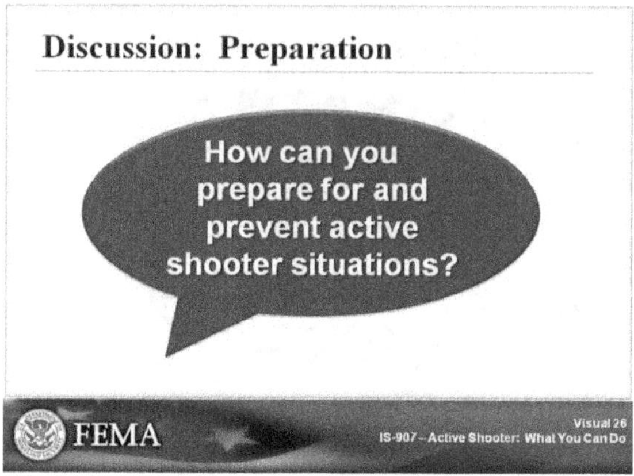

Key Points

What are some ways to prepare in advance for or prevent active shooter situations?

PREPARE

Visual 27

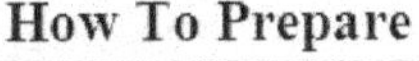
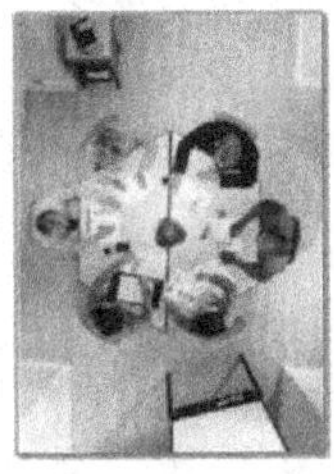

Key Points

Actions to take to prepare for and prevent potential active shooter incidents include:

- Developing an Emergency Action Plan.
- Conducting training.
- Recognizing indicators of potential workplace violence.

PREPARE

Visual 28

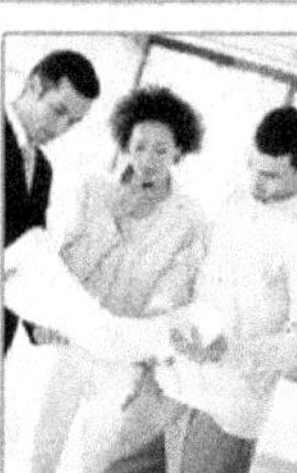

Key Points

The first step to prepare employees for an active shooter situation is to develop an Emergency Action Plan.

The Emergency Action Plan should include input from several stakeholders, including as applicable:

- The human resources department.
- The training department.
- The facility owners and/or operators.
- The property manager.
- Local law enforcement and emergency responders.

The Emergency Action Plan will identify measures that prepare employees to respond effectively and help minimize loss of life.

PREPARE

Visual 29

Key Points

An effective Emergency Action Plan includes the following:

- A preferred method for reporting different types of emergencies.
- An evacuation policy and procedure.
- Emergency escape procedures and route assignments (with floor plans and identification of designated safe areas).
- Contact information for—and responsibilities of—individuals to be contacted under the Emergency Action Plan.
- Information concerning local area hospitals (i.e., name, telephone number, and distance from your location).
- An emergency notification system to alert various parties of an emergency, including:
  - Individuals at remote locations within premises.
  - Local law enforcement.
  - Local area emergency responders and hospitals.

PREPARE

Visual 30

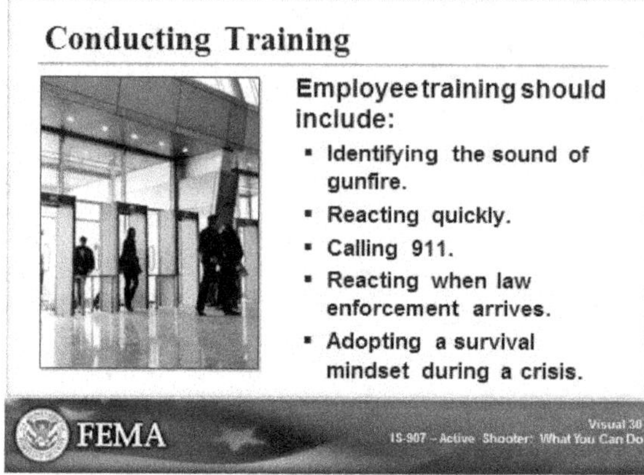

Key Points

Another important aspect of preparedness is training. The most effective way to train your employees to respond to an active shooter situation is to conduct mock active shooter training exercises. Local law enforcement organizations are an excellent resource in designing training exercises.

Employees should be trained in:

- Identifying the sound of gunfire.
- Reacting quickly when gunshots are heard or when a shooting is witnessed.
    - Evacuating the area
    - Hiding out
    - Acting against the shooter as a last resort
- Calling 911.
- Reacting when law enforcement arrives.
- Adopting a survival mindset during times of crisis.

For more information on training exercises, refer to IS-120.a: An Introduction to Exercises (http://training.fema.gov/EMIWeb/IS/IS120A.asp) and IS-130: Exercise Evaluation and Planning (http://training.fema.gov/EMIWeb/IS/IS130.asp).

PREPARE

Visual 31

Key Points

In addition to developing an Emergency Action Plan and conducting training, managers should ensure that:

- Plans, evacuation instructions, and any other relevant information include provisions for individuals with functional or other needs. For example, emergency signals should include both lights and sound and emergency exits should be accessible for persons with limited mobility.
- The facility is accessible for individuals with disabilities, in compliance with the requirements of the Americans with Disabilities Act (ADA).

PREPARE

Visual 32

Key Points

Facility managers should:

- Institute access controls (e.g., keys, security system passcodes).
- Distribute critical items to appropriate managers and employees, including:
  - Floor plans.
  - Keys and other access-control measures.
  - Facility personnel lists and telephone numbers.
  - Daily schedule.
- Assemble crisis kits containing:
  - Radios.
  - Floor plans.
  - Employee roster and emergency contact numbers.
  - First aid kits.
  - Flashlights.
- Activate the emergency notification system when an emergency situation occurs.
- Ensure that the facility has at least two evacuation routes.
- Coordinate with the facility's security department to ensure the physical security of the location.

(Continued on the following page.)

PREPARE

Visual 33

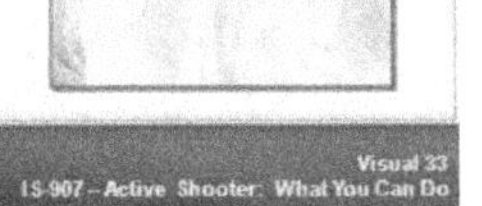

Key Points

Facility managers should also:

- Post evacuation routes in conspicuous locations throughout the facility.
- Place removable floor plans near entrances and exits for emergency responders.
- Include local law enforcement and first responders during training exercises.
- Encourage law enforcement, emergency responders, SWAT teams, canine teams, and bomb squads to train for an active shooter scenario at their location.
- Foster a respectful workplace.
- Be aware of indicators of workplace violence and take remedial actions accordingly.

PREPARE

Visual 34

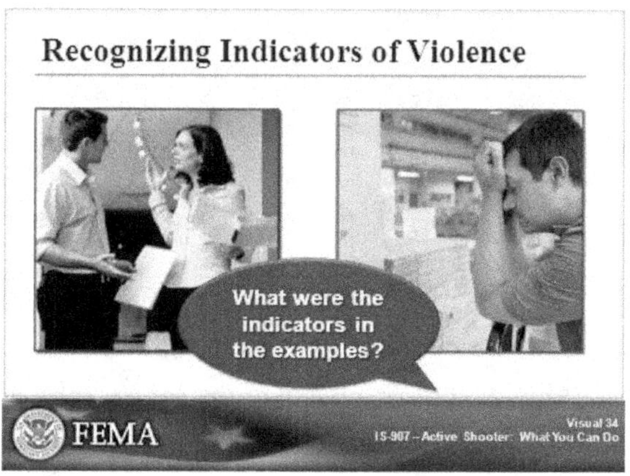

Key Points

Example 1:

Image 1.   Days before an office shooting at a software company, the shooter angrily confronted management over personal financial issues.

Image 2.   One member of payroll told her family that his behavior frightened her.

Image 3.   A few days later, the shooter asked two of his coworkers to witness the signing of his will.

Example 2:

Image 4.   The shooter at a warehouse incident was fired 6 months earlier for poor performance.

Image 5.   It was reported that he showed up late or missed entire days and was argumentative.

What indicators of potential violence did you note in the two examples?

PREPARE

Visual 35

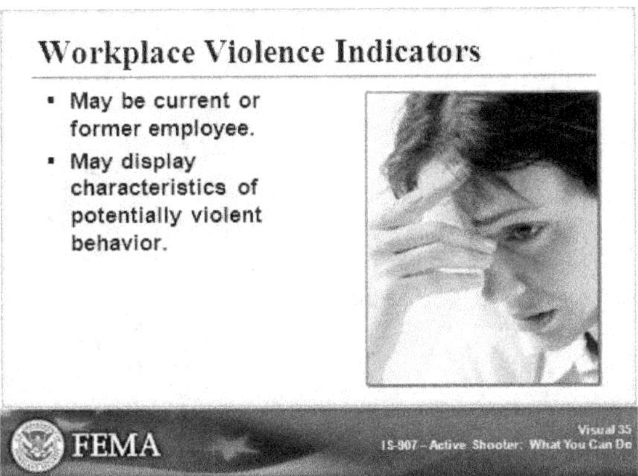

Key Points

An active shooter in your workplace may be a current or former employee, or an acquaintance of a current or former employee.

Intuitive managers and coworkers may notice characteristics of potentially violent behavior in an employee. Alert your supervisor or human resources department if you believe an employee or coworker exhibits potentially violent behavior.

PREPARE

Visual 36

Key Points

Your human resources department should engage in planning for emergency situations, including an active shooter scenario.

Planning for emergency situations can help to mitigate the likelihood of an incident by resulting in processes such as:

- Conducting effective employee screening and background checks.
- Creating a system for reporting signs of potentially violent behavior.
- Making counseling services available to employees.
- Developing an Emergency Action Plan that includes policies and procedures for dealing with an active shooter situation, as well as after-action planning.

ACTIVITY: INDICATORS OF WORKPLACE VIOLENCE

Visual 37

Key Points

Activity Purpose: To help you understand the indicators of potentially violent behavior.

Instructions: Working as a team:

1. Create a list of 10 indicators of potentially violent behavior.
2. Record the list on chart paper.
3. Select a spokesperson and be prepared to present your list in 5 minutes.

ACTIVITY: SELF-ASSESSMENT

Visual 38

Key Points

Activity Purpose: To help you assess the extent to which your organization has prepared for and worked to prevent active shooter situations, to identify where improvement is needed, and to identify steps for improvement that you can take following the training.

Instructions: Working individually:

1. Take 5 minutes to complete the self-assessment in your Student Manual.
2. Jot down action steps you can take for areas needing improvement.
3. Remember, this is a self-assessment, so be honest!

(Continued on the following page.)

ACTIVITY: SELF-ASSESSMENT

Visual 38 (Continued)

Has your organization . . .	Yes	No
Created a comprehensive Emergency Action Plan? Remember, the Emergency Action Plan should include:		
• A preferred method for reporting fires and other emergencies.	❏	❏
• An evacuation policy and procedure.	❏	❏
• Emergency escape procedures and route assignments (e.g., floor plans, safe areas).	❏	❏
• Contact information for—and responsibilities of—individuals to be contacted under the Emergency Action Plan.	❏	❏
• Information concerning local area hospitals (e.g., name, telephone number, and distance from your location).	❏	❏
• An emergency notification system to alert various parties of an emergency.	❏	❏
Ensured the presence of two emergency evacuation routes, and posted them in conspicuous locations?	❏	❏
Placed removable floor plans near entrances and exits for emergency responders?	❏	❏
Ensured that Emergency Action Plans and evacuation instructions address individuals with special needs and/or disabilities?	❏	❏
Ensured that your building is accessible for individuals with disabilities, and in compliance with the requirements of the Americans with Disabilities Act (ADA)?	❏	❏
Trained employees how to react to an active shooter scenario and other emergencies?	❏	❏
Conducted active shooter training exercises?	❏	❏
Coordinated with local law enforcement, emergency responders, SWAT teams, canine teams, and bomb squads in conducting exercises?	❏	❏
Conducted effective background checks for new employees?	❏	❏
Created a system for reporting potentially violent behavior?	❏	❏
Made counseling services available to employees?	❏	❏

FOLLOW UP

Visual 39

Key Points

This section covers followup actions to take after an active shooter incident.

FOLLOW UP

Visual 40

Key Points

Follow up actions after an actual incident include:

- Managing the consequences.
- Capturing lessons learned.

The results of taking follow up actions are:

- It promotes the well-being of those involved.
- It facilitates preparedness for future emergencies.

FOLLOW UP

Visual 41

Managing the Consequences

- Determine who is missing or injured.
- Determine a method for notifying families.
- Assess psychological state of individuals.
- Identify and fill critical personnel or operational gaps.

Key Points

After the active shooter has been incapacitated and is no longer a threat, human resources or management personnel should engage in post-event assessments and activities, including:

- An accounting of all individuals at a designated assembly point to determine if anyone is missing and potentially injured.
- Determining a method for notifying families of individuals affected by the active shooter, including notification of any casualties.
- Assessing the psychological state of individuals who were present at the scene, and referring them to health care specialists accordingly.
- Identifying and filling any critical personnel or operational gaps left in the organization as a result of the incident.

FOLLOW UP

Visual 42

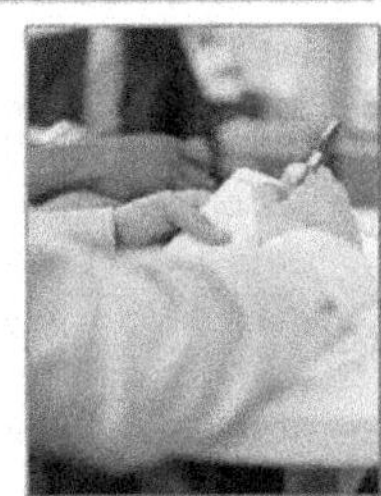

Key Points

To facilitate effective planning for future emergencies, it is important to analyze the recent active shooter situation and create an after-action report. The analysis and recommendations contained in this report are useful for:

- Serving as documentation for response activities.
- Identifying successes and failures that occurred during the event.
- Providing an analysis of the effectiveness of the existing Emergency Action Plan.
- Describing and defining a plan for making improvements to the Emergency Action Plan.

ACTIVITY: POST-EVENT ACTIONS

Visual 43

Key Points

Activity Purpose: To help you understand how best to follow up after an active shooter incident occurs.

Instructions: Working as a team:

1. Review the scenario in the Student Manual.
2. Write a list of post-event actions you should take the day of an active shooter incident and in the coming weeks.
3. Select a spokesperson and be prepared to present your list in 5 minutes.

Scenario:

On a quiet morning, a former employee comes in through the front entrance of your office building and immediately opens fire. The manager guides employees to a preplanned evacuation route while others who are stuck in the room hide. Hearing sirens, the former employee runs back out to the parking lot, where he is arrested in a matter of minutes. Two shots were fired, and two people were injured, but law enforcement has informed you that there is no longer a threat.

FOLLOW UP

Visual 44

Key Points

You may find the following resources helpful in preparing for and preventing active shooter incidents:

- **Active Shooter Desk Reference Guide** (http://www.dhs.gov/xlibrary/assets/active_shooter_booklet.pdf): This booklet provides guidance to individuals, including managers and employees, who become involved in an active shooter situation, and discusses how to react when law enforcement responds.
- **Active Shooter Pocket-Sized Reference Card** (http://www.dhs.gov/xlibrary/assets/active_shooter_pocket_card.pdf): This guide provides a brief overview of how best to respond to an active shooter situation.
- **Active Shooter Poster** (http://www.dhs.gov/xlibrary/assets/active_shooter_poster.pdf): This poster describes how to respond to an active shooter, as well as how to recognize signs of potential workplace violence.

Active shooter materials help managers, employees, training staff, and human resources personnel mitigate the risk of, and take appropriate action in response to, an active shooter situation.

These and other retail training resources can be found at the:
- **Department of Homeland Security Commercial Facilities Web site** (http://www.dhs.gov/files/programs/gc_1259859901230.shtm).
- **FEMA Emergency Management Institute (EMI) Independent Study Program Web site** (http://training.fema.gov/is/crslist.asp).

The following page lists additional resources.

FOLLOW UP

Visual 44 (Continued)

- **Commercial Facilities Sector Training and Resources** (http://www.dhs.gov/files/programs/gc_1259859901230.shtm): This Web site provides various resources for the Commercial Facilities Sector, including three courses, links to subsector tools and webinars, and informational videos.
- **IS-120.a An Introduction to Exercises** (http://training.fema.gov/EMIWeb/IS/IS120A.asp): This course introduces the basics of emergency management exercises and builds a foundation for subsequent exercise courses, which provide the specifics of the Homeland Security Exercise and Evaluation Program (HSEEP).
- **IS-130 Exercise Evaluation and Design** (http://training.fema.gov/EMIWeb/IS/IS130.asp): This course introduces the basics of emergency management exercise evaluation and improvement planning.
- **Lessons Learned Information Sharing** (http://www.llis.gov/): This information and collaboration resource serves as the national, online network of lessons learned, best practices, and innovative ideas for the emergency management and homeland security communities.
- **Safety Guidelines for Armed Subjects, Active Shooter Situations, Indiana University Police Department (April 2007)** (http://129.79.26.55/orm/SiteMap2.cfm?todo=HandbookArmed): This document provides an overview of how to respond to varying active shooter scenarios, as well as what to expect from responding police officers.
- **Safety Tips and Guidelines Regarding Potential "Active Shooter" Incidents Occurring on Campus, University of California Police** (http://ucpd.ucla.edu/070402CP.pdf): This document defines an active shooter and provides tips and guidelines for responding to active shooter scenarios.
- **Shots Fired, When Lightning Strikes (DVD), Center for Personal Protection and Safety (2007)** (http://www.shotsfireddvd.com/): This DVD provides strategies to prevent and survive active shooter situations.
- **How to Plan for Workplace Emergencies and Evacuations, U.S. Department of Labor, Occupational Health and Safety Administration, OSHA 3088 (2001)** (http://www.osha.gov/Publications/osha3088.pdf): This booklet provides a general overview of dealing with emergency situations, including developing an evacuation plan, training employees, and utilizing resources.
- **The Active Shooter Awareness Virtual Roundtable** (Webinar), Department of Homeland Security (2011) (https://connect.hisn.gov/asaware2011): This roundtable will better prepare you to deal with an active shooter situation and to recognize dangerous behavior before it turns deadly.

COURSE SUMMARY

Visual 45

Key Points

In the event of an active shooter situation:

- Evacuate
  - o Attempt to evacuate
  - o Have an escape route and plan
  - o Leave your belongings
  - o Keep your hands visible
- Hide
  - o Find a place to hide
  - o Block entry and lock doors
  - o Remain quiet and silence your cell phone or pager
- Take Action
  - o As a last resort, try to incapacitate the shooter
  - o Act with physical aggression

CALL 911 WHEN IT IS SAFE TO DO SO!

Remember to always:

- Take note of the two nearest exits in any facility you visit.
- Be aware of your environment and any possible dangers.

COURSE SUMMARY

Visual 46

Key Points

1. Take a few moments to review your Student Manual and identify any questions.
2. Ensure that all questions are answered.
3. When taking the test . . .

- Read each item carefully.
- Enter the answers online.

You may refer to the Student Manual when completing the test.

To receive a certificate of completion, you must take the 12-question multiple-choice exam and achieve a score of 75%.

If desired, you may download and print the course exam and circle your responses on the paper copy before entering them online. The online exam questions and responses, however, are randomly generated and may not match the order presented in the printable copy.

You must complete your tests online. Certificates will be sent electronically to the email address entered during registration.

To complete the course exam:

- Go to the **IS-907 – Active Shooter: What You Can Do** course (http://training.fema.gov/EMIWeb/IS/IS907.asp).
- Click on "Take Final Exam."

COURSE SUMMARY

Visual 47

Key Points

This page intentionally left blank.

9 781979 877787